Real Communal Commerce

*How to Make Millions and Start a Movement
by Serving Others*

By **Brian Desind**

ISBN 979 870570 1384

Cover Design by Michael Williams

@sedatedhypestudios

Contributing Editor Ofelia Desind

Dedicated to my amazing wife, Ofelia, my daughter Elle and every member of Privada Cigar Club, past and present, without whom none of this would be possible.

#weareprivada

There is no business without the consumers that support them. With this mantra in mind, it is time to change the way we look at capitalism and how we serve the people who are the entire reason the business exists in the first place.

Foreword

If you want to create a successful business, read this book! And do not speed read. I cut out all the fat and only left in the important information, so read every word slowly. You can still finish this book quickly, I promise!

I'll get started with some quick fundamentals. There are a few things I think you should know before reading this book. First and foremost: what I refer to as Real Communal Commerce has made me more successful, more quickly than any of my other business endeavors combined.

Before even that, let me introduce myself. My name is Brian Desind. I was a singer/songwriter for most of my life. I've had multiple record deals and about a thousand uniquely crappy jobs along the way, just trying to keep that dream alive. I've worked for the largest companies and the smallest mom and pop shops. From Apple to banking to bartending to sales... I have done it all. I was the world's worst employee, and I'm possibly the world's best millennial entrepreneur (after 40 years of typing I finally spelled that word right, first try without spell check, go me! You have to celebrate the small wins).

Anyway, back to business. I have seen large financial firms boom and bust, and small and medium sized businesses thrive and fail, too. The failures have been almost more important than the wins and that's something that's vital to remember as someone trying to learn the ropes. So, if you have failed at business in the past, congratulations! You are on your way. I didn't start really finding true success until I learned how to harness the power and potential of the people around me. COMMUNITY. So that's what I'm going to focus on in the following pages.

The first concept you will need to embrace is becoming COMMUNITY focused. Think about who your clientele is, and find out what they want! It's a simple concept that seems to have gotten lost in the mental gymnastics of contemporary business. The power of community is so great and so rewarding, you might not believe the difference it can make in your life before it starts happening. But keep your ear to the ground, and keep an open mind. This is the biggest takeaway.

The second thing you need to know is that I used the Communal Commerce protocol in an industry that is hated, overtaxed, and damn near outlawed federally and in most states. I never imagined it would be this successful. I simply wanted to get the products I loved at a discount, and maybe make a few dollars along the way. What ensued inspired me to write this book and share this new business model with all of you. If I have been able to watch my business flourish in an industry that is frowned upon, barely profitable, and possibly soon to be extinct, you can do it in almost any industry with greater ease.

Thirdly, I had no funding or loans to create the business, and I have no debt. I firmly believe that small to medium sized businesses should require very little debt. Do not dig yourself into a hole. With Communal Commerce, in most cases you will grow with your audience. This is an opportunity to start small, and to plant seeds. Seeds are cheap! But the seeds will grow, and your business will grow with them. You just have to invest by nurturing the seeds, and paying attention to what they need in order to flourish. You see where I'm going with this.

Fourth, I think Communal Commerce works fastest, not better, necessarily, but fastest, with two added ingredients: niche and passion. Finding a niche gives you a clearer target as to who you are servicing. Passion for your craft or product is important, but should not be great enough to force you to make bad decisions like refinancing your house for your dream of becoming a coffee roaster or race car driver. Follow? Here is a quick example of finding your niche. Let's say you are a roofer. Every house has a roof so who the hell do you start marketing to, and how? Terra-cotta roofs are a pain in the ass. You know how to patch terra-cotta roofs. You learn everything you can about them and now you are the terra-cotta roof company. Every terra-cotta roof you pass by, stop and let them know you are a terra-cotta roof specialist. Makes sense. This gives you a niche which gives you a focus.

As an important side note, I want you to know that Communal Commerce works for any company as long as your product or service is mostly predictable. In a broker-style business where you subcontract work to other people, this may not work, and could actually backfire because of its social nature. You have to invest the time to build these relationships yourself.

Lastly, I need you to know a few quick facts about me so you know I'm not some self-proclaimed, millennial business guru who just needs another $49.95 to unlock the last part of this process. I'm giving you everything you need to know in order to be successful right here. I am the founder of Privada Cigar Club, an exclusive premium cigar club that ships its members packages of rare and hard to find cigars. I make about 15,000 people very happy every single month. Although it is a business, it is also a whole lot more than that. It is a community that I built using the principles of Communal Commerce outlined in this book. This community also happened to be my most successful business endeavor to date, as well as the most fun and rewarding one by far. It's a passion project, a lively community, and a renewing and sustainable business. It's also a repeatable model, and I'm excited to share the concepts I used to achieve my dreams with YOU! Throughout the book I will even include a few emails I've received over the years so you can see the impact communal commerce business makes on peoples' lives every day. Last names and email addresses were omitted for their privacy, of course. But the people and their stories are as genuine as it gets.

I'm almost done I promise. Let's talk about you and the things that will be vital, or at the very least, helpful along the way. YOU need to be a good communicator, a better listener, and a person with integrity (with yourself AND your customers) to employ the Communal Commerce practices. You do not need funding, a formal education, or any other skills in particular. If you have a business already, awesome. If you are just starting or want to start a business, awesome. You can employ the strategies of Communal Commerce at any stage in your business. You should be able to use your laptop like a samurai uses swords, be willing to really listen to the people around you, and to be able to communicate well through your writing. That does not mean you never make grammatical errors, it just means that you can get your point across through email and social media. You have to be genuine with people too, because they can smell fakes from a mile away. The best way to do this is by understanding how VALUABLE their opinions are.

As digital commerce continues to become the

dominant venue of business of the future in just about any industry, the importance of personalized communication and fostering REAL relationships will become more and more crucial. Nobody wants to be isolated, even if all of their socializing, shopping, and work is done from home! So, how do we fill the void of REAL community in a digital age? Communal Commerce is the future of how business will be done in America. Communal Commerce is not social media, although social medial can be a tool of its employ. It's starting a conversation with the people you serve, and continuing that conversation until you build a community. It's listening. It's SERVING. It's leveraging your knowledge of your community's desires into a movement.

The steps outlined in this book are titled Serve, Engage, Authoritize, Excite, and Expand. These steps will guide you through the processes and strategies involved in transitioning your new, or existing business, into the Communal Commerce method!

If you like the idea of making big money, and most importantly making peoples' lives better, keep reading. When you are done, I want to hear from you.

YES, you. If you don't email me, you didn't get enough out of this book. I'll give you my email address and maybe even try to help you along your journey. I do not care how large or small your business is, either. I believe the world can be a much better place and Communal Commerce is going to spark a cultural change. It's already happening. Now, without further ado, get ready to make friends, build a movement, and make money along the way with a new style of business. Welcome to the world of Communal Commerce! .

Contents

Chapter 1

Serve. Don't Just Sell.

This is possibly the most important idea you will need to grasp from this book. Serve. It's so simple. Yet big businesses don't think like this yet. Our culture is self-serving. YOU want to be rich. YOU are focused on your desires and needs.

Well, the reality is YOU are a dick, and that way of thinking is a great way to run yourself in circles and get nothing out of it. Don't feel bad, society programs us to be this way. It's just today's culture. Self serve. You don't need anyone. You have the internet. You have your phone. Community in your family and town have almost gone completely to shit. And boy oh boy, nobody is handing out lifeline favors anymore, right? So fuck them…that's largely the sentiment these days. My father used to tell me to try and find a guy who will retire in the next 5-10 years and be a star employee. Maybe he'll sell or leave you the business some day. That used to happen. That was probably when people knew each other though. When community, in-person, face-to-face contact was a real thing. I'm honestly unsure wether I'm painting this picture better or worse than it really is, but this is reality now. It is what it is— The most dry saying of all time. But I digress. The point is, it is not your fault, you did not create the current social climate, but, you can use this climate to your benefit and shine like the star YOU know you are. As I mentioned earlier, there is a shift in culture happening, and you are a part of that now. Here is how to get your head in the right mindset. DO THE OPPOSITE! Ah man, it's astonishing just how simple the best things in life really are. Aside from rose gold Rolexes and Teslas of course. Or whatever self-serving items are on your desires, lists and vision boards. But think about it. What if it's truly this simple. Do what others are not doing. I guess, in this case, that would mean serving others, rather than serving yourself.

Now, let me tell you, ladies and gentlemen, I was a self server. Holy shit. I ate it, smoked it, drank it, wore it, drove it and did everything I could to make more and more money to self serve like the best of them. I didn't realize the actual way to do this was a mindset shift. So don't go thinking I'm better than you. My intelligence lies in my ability to perceive reality, and live there, even at its depths, taking serious notes on every angle I can possibly see it from. I've been fortunate to make all the mistakes I've made because I've learned from every single one of them! To me, there would be nothing more arrogant than to achieve success without understanding how it happened. Everything in this book is based on my own analysis of my success in a Communal Commerce business. I profited millions of dollars in a very short period of time and more importantly, and I can't stress this enough when I say MORE IMPORTANTLY, MADE PEOPLE HAPPY! Here I am, this elder millennial, (which I believe was important in my understanding of this concept of Communal Commerce), a self-serving person, just like everyone else telling you that in regards to securing a future for my family, money was not the important part,

3

but the thing that brought me the most joy, and has created a legacy that I am truly proud of, is MAKING OTHER PEOPLE HAPPY. I may have happened to make a bit of profit along the way. And how did I do this?

I served my people.

And let me tell you something, you greedy piece of shit, nobody has served their people like me since I don't know when. If you even attempt to serve your members, clients, consumers, constituents (if this is your case you are truly fucked up...kidding, kidding) partners, family and friends the way I serve the members of my Privada Community, you will be a true success with WEALTH not just riches. And guess what, there is a big difference between those two things. Rich is lonely. Wealth is shared.

Let's take a moment to digest this theoretic prophecy I have laid upon you. How can you best serve? Does serving others make you feel bad? Good? Has serving others in the past left you feeling unappreciated? Does it make you feel vulnerable? Don't worry about any possible negative feelings that come up when you think about serving others. I don't think you have grasped the concept fully yet.

Before we do that, let's look at some examples of how business is done these days in most situations and companies.

Maybe I'm biased, but I see Privada as one of the most progressive and futuristic styles of business that exists right now. It's possibly the ground zero of Communal Commerce, and I believe it is truly the future of ALL business, particularly in free countries. My company is profitable and has been from its inception. If any of you have MBAs or come from Dot Com culture— you have been taught that in the beginning, you invest and invest and invest- from hiring the best talent to snagging the hottest real estate space, to getting the best coffee makers for that best talent you hired. Then you get to work in a shit ton of debt and hope and pray that by years two or three, your company starts to become profitable. That's bullshit. In this business model, we were never in debt and guess what, by year two we were seeing profits in the millions.

The best part is, I'm getting my members a discount on products they would have been consuming anyway. I'm preparing and reviewing the products for them, adding value to their experience, and I'm tailoring the experience and products to my members' wants and desires. Let me summarize this, I'm making profits AND my customers and members are getting greater value than they would with any of my so called competitors. Competitors..ha…as if. More like self-serving commodity vultures that think volume is the way to build business. But hey, I can't blame them for doing things the way they have always been done. And, although it could potentially take some of our consumers away, I would teach this to any of them that would put it to use. I think Communal Commerce has the potential to fix a lot of the problems we all see in corporate America, and to make the world just a little bit better. Plus, I truly believe that there is room for everyone in a Communal Commerce world. Competitors don't matter when your product or service is unique to you and the way you do things.

Let me say that again: The reason for your success is YOU. You are what makes your business unique. This means that if your competition doesn't have you they cannot do what YOU do. If you are employing the practices in this book, you're going to carve out a unique part of a market just for you. Community Commerce. Get in where you fit in. In order to do this you need to have a few things under your belt. Ladies, get your pencils ready.

First, you have to have an interest something, or at least have the desire to delve into that interest. Or maybe you can just recognize a good niche. We can all bring a unique perspective to things here. This is going to seriously help you narrow down business ideas. Narrowing down business ideas for aspiring startup owners can shave years off your success story. If some Wall Street business tycoon in an expensive suit had gotten into the backseat of my black car when I was a chauffeur and said, "Hey idiot, stop thinking about what business to start, you can only start a business in the industry of "flibiddyjibits," it would would have saved me years of time narrowing my focus to flibiddyjibbits, rather than a world of anything. There is something to be said about a small menu. Now, on the flip side, I also believe that leaning too heavily into a particular passion to the point of being blind to the interests of your business and its feasibility is a sure-fire way to kill your entrepreneurial dreams. What I mean is this: passion-driven businesses that lose sight of money entirely can fail, and fail hard. I once met a loan officer who went on to become a successful cartoonist say that he was not allowed to lend money to people with passion-based business ideas. Their passions make them vulnerable to bad business decisions and they typically hemorrhage capital and lose their funding. So let's not do that. Figure out what you're in this for. Let's go with something we are into. Hobby style. So we can keep our business head in the game, but still balance that with genuine knowledge and passion!

I was really into cigars. Start with something that you'll be purchasing anyway. It will save you money if you are the one buying at wholesale rates and then selling enough to cover your costs, at least. Let's say you are a clothing junkie, and your hobby is buying all the best brands every season. Becoming a retailer of the clothing brands you love will allow you to buy those brands at wholesale prices which means your personal expenses will be cut back, saving you money. Or if you are a little bit of a lush, you can figure out a way to legally buy wine and spirits at wholesale cost and resell those spirits at a profit. And, you get your spirits for way less than you did before. Make sense?

So, let's say you're a musician. Instead of obsessing over making your first album, a smarter approach is to start with creating a digital music distribution network or platform that allows you to sell music and create a crowd for your platform. Once that platform is successful at somehow getting people to pay for music (this was a bad example...) maybe then, you can create that album and you will already have paying consumers to distribute it to. You have also served your fellow musicians by creating a space for them to sell their music.

See, becoming a recording artist was only important to you and served you most. By helping people find a niche genre of music and helping the other musicians in that niche connect with an audience, you created a way to serve these people that will in turn serve you when you finally do drop that album. There is a lot more to it than this, but this is a good way to get you thinking in the right direction.

You have to be looking to serve others, not just yourself. This can be hard on the ego, but it's important to be honest with yourself. So while you should be selfish in choosing a business or product that you are genuinely interested in, and can personally vouch for, the business should not serve only your desires. It should channel your desires in a way that serves others, and benefits you along the way.

Again, I liked cigars. More importantly I liked rare cigars. I also did not want to make my own cigars, at least not then. There is a great freaking point, actually. Let's digress a moment. Had I set out to make my own cigars, I possibly would have failed or not even been able to get started. Or worse, been semi-successful and just been another brand in an industry filled with brands. Do you have any idea how many people try to start their own cigar brand each year?

What is it that I do instead? I curate rare cigars. I put them in a box and ship them to my members' doors each month. I also write a review along with pairing notes and tasting notes and even include a story about each cigar and how those cigars found themselves in the box. It is not only a great cigar smoking experience that did not exist before Privada, but it is also is the single best cigar education a cigar smoker could ever ask for. I serve people who are looking for rare cigars. I serve people who are looking to learn about cigars. I get my members access to cigars made by the smaller, hard to find cigar manufacturers and farms that make the best cigars in the world but that did not get the attention they deserved prior to Privada.

So let's talk about how this works, in real world examples. We serve others two different ways. Before me, some of the manufacturers were rarely talked about. I figured out how to use the Privada momentum to help them, while they helped us. Let's call this type of serving *back serving*. While back serving worked for me, I'm not sure it was necessary but it sure helped me establish a certain reputation and vibe, and secure some good connections along the way. Other people in my industry laughed at me. "Why would he mention this factory or that farm? Those guys are nobodies." That kind of thing. So I believe it created good juju in the vibes department (vibes bruh) and eventually the cost of goods department because SURPRISE! Everyone wants to work with a distributor that makes them famous in their field.

Another important side note, do not study all of

your potential competition to a point of exhaustion. Do not get an idea and then start looking for other companies that already do it. This, my friends, is IDEA KILLER madness. Comparison is the thief of joy (and originality!) If you know you want to approach a business differently, then what difference does it make who does it already, and what they're doing? There were, and still are, other cigar subscriptions out there. But they are not Privada, and Privada is not them. The other clubs just sent people regular cigars you can find at any shop. They did serve their people in the sense of value. This is where baby boomers focused a lot of their energy: volume, cost-cutting, and value only in a monetary sense.

Millennials and beyond, for better or worse, find value not only in the cost of goods, but in the way those goods or services are marketed to them, and how they are experienced. This is something only the wealthy really captured before this generation. People with so much money to blow that they had to create ways to spend it all. Craft beer benefited tremendously from this shift in culture. Luxury brands are killing it because of this as well. Meanwhile, the presentation of the experiences of these things remains lackluster.

These businesses could truly push these brands over the top in regards to success and brand loyalty. There is a lot of untapped gold there. More of that later. As I write this, it's Christmas break 2020 (FUCK YOU 2020). We are all stuck at home, or stuck at work and then stuck at home without much of an escape valve for fun. I'm doing some soul searching, myself.

The conversation goes something like this: "Self, what are you hungry for?"

Self replies "A great hamburger, because I just finished a keto diet and some greasy protein and carbohydrates would really do the trick."

I have a plethora of options, but for quick service I'll give you the popular choices. McDonalds for a Big Mac meal at $5.99 which comes with the double burger, fries, and a soda (I just checked their website because I thought it cost more than this). Or, Five Guys at $7.99 for the cheese burger (also a double), fries at $4 and a drink for $2 a total of $13.99.

Ask a young person which place they want to go to next time they ask for a burger and fries. If they've had both, most will say Five Guys. My father, who is the embodiment of the term baby boomer in every way, will knock Five Guys. He will say something like, "It's not that great! It's too expensive!"

Or, "but I loved the peanuts. Do they even still do the peanuts?" When it was new to him he justified the price of the meal with the free peanuts. GENIUS IDEA!

So why does the young person want the Five Guys over McDonalds? And no, if you are guessing they're stealing the free peanuts, that's not it. I know one thing, it's not about the value as a price. They pay more than double at Five Guys because it's about the experience. What do I like about Five Guys? The quality and the place. Starbucks, same thing. Young people are still showing up at Starbucks in epic numbers all across the world. In fact, in some cities Starbucks is the coolest place to hang out (shout out to Allentown, Pennsylvania!)

When Howard Schultz started Starbucks, he wanted his coffee shop to be the third place people spent most time in after home and work. Some of these people don't even like coffee that much, and they sure as hell weren't behind my father in line at the gas station to get coffee before Starbucks came to town. Now Starbucks is a meeting place, a study hall and a makeshift conference room for millions of people all over the world every day. Same thing with In-and-Out Burger. In-and-Out is unique because it gives you value and experience and has a line down the block at all times of day (an ironic twist to their name, if you ask me). It's all about the EXPERIENCE.

Allow me to serve you through experience. What's the best way to communicate experience? How can you communicate experience through story telling? I've heard some people in my industry say nasty things about me. One thing I've heard them say is that I'm making up stories about products. I hate to hurt them even more than they already are, but the stories are fact. But the stories weren't always sexy at face value, so you have to look deeply, think narratively, and search for the facts that make the best story. We can come back to that. This is about experience. Show me. Tell me. Write me. Submerse me. Immerse me! Get ready for that next. Immersive experience. From the moment you walk in, or enter the website, every facet of your experience is intentional.

Back to our burger metaphor, because now I'm hungry. I walk into a certain fast food establishment we're all familiar with (no need for naming names), and that shit is nasty 90% of the time. Ketchup on the counters, a straw wrapper sticking to my foot, and the cashiers are rolling their eyes at me. I walk into Five Guys and it's clean. It's retro, it has style, I can see the people working hard to make my meal right. I pick the ingredients and build the burger, I get my choice of seasoned or classic fries, and they package it in a brown bag like an elementary school lunch, which I personally love. That sounds way more fun and delicious than going to You Know Who and getting screamed at, "NEXT! ORDER! WE DON'T HAVE THAT!"

No matter how hard you work at building relationships with your customers, it will only go half as far if your employees are overworked and underpaid. It always shows in the end result. Most fast food employees look upset. I don't know what Five Guys pays employees, but I don't get that vibe from Five Guys quite as much. The service is just as much a part of the experience as the VALUE. In fact, good service *is* valuable. A lot of the time, you can even take money out of the equation. People are not as cheap as they used to be. A personal aside: I can't stand cheap people. There's a difference between broke and cheap. If you need to be frugal, do it! But cheap..for what? YOLO!

Let's bring another example into the mix. I love shopping at Costco. We all do. They are another place that nails you with both experience and value. Yeah, folks like my my dad are there too, eating all the samples they can get their hands on, plus a hot dog on the way out. They shop there and they keep coming back. What adds to that experience, however, is the warehouse effect and the employees. They are happy! They get paid well. WOW. A company that pays well. Do you know what happens when you pay well? We will come back to this, but I do want to tell you one key factor I left out of my introduction to my version of Communal Commerce. I rarely go the office. This means I can focus my energy on the most important parts of the business, and my people make sure the machine keeps running. MY people work their asses off. Not out of fear. Not out of pressure. But because I take time to search for and hire the right people, I pay well, and I leave them alone, but they know I'm approachable if there's an issue. I let them know they are appreciated. I visit my warehouse twice a week at best. The place runs by itself. Again, we will come back to this part, but I swear my cigars taste better because my people are happy. Believe or not, businesses run better when the employees are happy. Things run smoothly, and there are fewer fires to put out. You can spend your energy as a business owner planning for the future instead of playing catchup. I'm almost at the point where I will consider an employee owned business for my next venture. Happiness adds to the experience!

Anyway. For me the real opportunity lies in offering your clientele both discount and experience. We all know companies who rely strictly on experience and charge astronomically for their goods (shout out to Rolex and all the overly expensive luxury brands that don't engage with their consumers.) Sure, you can get three crappy cigars for about two thirds of the price from the other guys, but you can't get *these* three cigars and you can't get this experience. And this is truly better than that, on multiple levels. So my club was a lot like the Five Guys compared to McDonalds option, but we threw a little In-and-Out and Costco in the game too.

So just imagine this: giving your customers the best of both worlds. The best experience for a great value. Game over for the competition. You want to serve your potential clients as best as possible. This means your experience will be a good one for a number of different reasons. So how will you best serve your people? How can you make sure you not only met your customer's initial needs, but that you continue to do so as their taste and your business grow?

So in conclusion. How?? How do you begin to serve others? Start by understanding the things you want from a product or service and how awesome it would be if someone did these things for you when they sold you a product or service. Start or continue your business with these things in mind. You are not so unique (sorry). What would make you a happy and satisfied customer will make others happy too. If you were the customer what would knock your socks off? Do that and then even more importantly, once you have customers to serve, you want to SPEAK to them and find out what else you can offer them. Yes, actually

SPEAK to your customers! Holy shit!! I know its an audacious idea but if you want to serve people to the fullest you're going to have to engage them! Which takes us to our next chapter.

From:
Date: Wed, Dec 9, 2020 at 1:59 PM
Subject: Thank you
To: Privada Cigar Club <info@privadacigarclub.com>

Dear Team Privada

I wanted to convey my deepest gratitude on all levels, it's difficult to know where to start, but during these unsettling times you have brought a great deal of energy, entertainment, advice and friendship to the world of cigars.

Your YouTube channel brings so much accessibility, it's like sitting down with your buddies and chewing the fat, talking about your passion and how to enjoy those moments cigars bring.

The opportunity to learn and get great cigars, the kind you want to share with good friends and savour the experiences what great artisan products bring, and you're so inclusive to all that show a great love of cigars.

The way your treat us as customers is a credit to your ideals, I thank you all for that. it makes me feel valued and I love it.

Keep doing what you do. May your wishes come true

You have been a ray of sunshine during COVID and my work at the hospital can be all consuming, you give me an opportunity to escape. I thank you deeply for that.
Peace to you all
And may 2021 be rocking

Ian

"Customer service should not just be a department. It should be the entire company."

Tony Hsieh

CEO, Zappos

Chapter 2

Engage. Don't Ignore.

Areal communal commerce business is a dialogue, not a monologue. Non communal commerce, monologue style businesses will slowly fade away in this next generation of entrepreneurialism. People aren't necessarily going to want what you think they want, and it's your job to find out what it is that they REALLY want. I've learned this one the hard way. It's not always going to be glamorous.

The first thing that comes to mind in this category is an experience I had in a previous career as a singer/songwriter. I was a big city kid who really believed I was only going to achieve fame or success in one particular way: writing what I hoped to be hit records and getting the attention of a major record label that would make me a star. Looking back now, I see how ridiculous that is, but this was right at the advent of the MP3 and prior to this pivotal moment, that was the way a lot of artists got out there.

I'm telling you this because when I finally figured out how to make money from my music, I was already 30 years old, CDs were dead and I had to hit the road and work for the money. I opened for acts that may have had one popular song 10 years prior and made a living touring ever since. I also met other middle acts that never had any songs on the radio but made quite a good living hitting the towns no one else wanted to go. Places like Casper, Wyoming. These guys understood the hustle in a way that I did not back then. They carved out their own corner of the market and they gave the people what they wanted, when others would not. Instead of vying for spots in big cities and working their fingers to the bone for nothing, they found what worked in their reality. Anyway, back to Casper. I was chatting with a guy at a show there, freezing my ass off outside the venue, wondering why in the hell anyone would bother to show up that night. When I asked this guy why he came to the show that night he replied by telling me he had two choices: "It was either this, or midget wrestling."

My mentality then was "Damn that is very uncool. I won't be coming back to Casper…"

What I think now is "Casper is an untapped market that will SHOW UP if you give them a chance, and there isn't much competition." Isn't it amazing what a simple change of perspective and a decade or so of wisdom can do?

My big city wannabe rockstar ego was not at all interested in the types of people that came to our shows. I was ready for hot chicks and cool parties. What we experienced was quite possibly the diametric opposite. I didn't realize that the not-so-glamorous networks I could have built then had the potential to be valuable to my goals. Due to my lack of experience, I totally let seeds die. I was nice to people, and even kept in touch with a few, but what could have been with a little extra ground work is extraordinary. One thing I found out quickly was that you did not need talent to do well in the touring circuit. So the entire thing was upside down for me and my big city arrogance. I didn't see the value and missed out. I'm glad I did though, because it is truly an unhealthy lifestyle. Hindsight is always 20/20!

These are the types of lessons and experiences I always kept in the back of my mind, especially during the early stages of Privada Cigar Club. I LISTENED to people from the get go. Remember this, even if it's the only thing you take away from this book: Treat every single relationship, and I mean every single one, you create through your business or craft like a seedling. It has great energy if planted properly and can blossom into something that is actually quite rare these days. Connection. Community. TRUE FRIENDSHIP. And the reason for this is situational. You can engineer *your* business to facilitate this type of connection.

Imagine how easy it would be to get along with some of your non work friends if they respected you as a successful person and potential authority in your shared craft or hobby. Friendship levels up. That respect, if returned mutually, can create the beginnings of an incredibly strong businesses foundation. A well laid foundation is priceless and will help you build something that can last.

By giving your customers a platform to socialize

on, events to attend (either in person or virtual) and a way to find friendship within that community, you can create a lasting momentum based around your product or service. Every member or customer should be treated like an influential person in your company's success story, especially the early adapters. These folks should be treated like future best friends. In the earlier stages of your company you have absolutely nothing more valuable to do with your time than to serve these people and to make them fall in love with your brand's experience. Talk about a return on investment, you schmuck.

I consider ALL of my club members my friends. We share a hobby, and we help each other enjoy the best that the hobby has to offer. The members I have gotten to communicate with the most even more so. I spend A LOT of my time communicating with my friends and members in Privada. This is something I truly enjoy, and it's had great benefits for the business, too. I know immediately HOW my decisions are going over with my clientele. There is no red tape separating us. I know what they're enjoying and I know what could be improved upon. And my members know that I am listening to them! Corporate types call this a focus group, but I can't stress to you enough what a waste of time and money it would be to get people like this in a group setting and not become their friends.

I encourage this communication through engagement. Imagine this. Let's say Eminem puts out a new documentary. The catch is, he's not allowing the big streaming services to sell or stream it. You have to buy this documentary direct from Em on his website. When Eminem sells through Apple he makes 10% or maybe even 50%. But when he sells through his website he makes 100%. So he can sell less numbers yet still make as much or more profits. This is extremely important to keep in mind, friends. Margin. Lean, mean and meaningful. I'll take 100 loyal, repeat customers over 10,000, fleeting one time customers any day of the week. Two days after you stream Em's documentary, you get an email from Em himself thanking you for your purchase. Not a bot, actually from the REAL Slim Shady. You start a conversation, or as I refer to it, you nurture the initial sprouting of the seed.

This is the first REAL engagement. It is possibly the most meaningful. This is where you need to give that seed everything it requires to grow. Some seeds need a little more time and TLC than others, but the basic rule of thumb is that if you can get this right, you can win long term. Every season this seed will yield.

Right now, most businesses are basically grabbing the yield and ditching the plant. A lot of those plants won't grow again next year. When we think about a successful business, we think of a sustainable business that can last through the years. The allure of immediate gain through cutting corners only ends up destroying the foundation you have worked so hard to build! These quick cash grab companies aren't going to be a part of our American landscape for much longer. These businesses are so focused on growing quickly that they waste their time looking for new seeds rather than fostering these plants to grow again.

So, I ask you to imagine this with me. Which farmer would you prefer to be in this situation? Farmer A is always on the hunt looking for new seeds and strains of seeds to grow his produce each year. He grows the produce and does pretty well but boy does he hustle his ass off all winter looking for more seeds. Farmer B planted seeds the first few seasons but he figured out a way to nurture the plants so that they grow back each year, without having to plant more seeds. He doesn't have to ever buy new seeds again, and he gets to stay warm all winter, cozied up in his home with his family and friends. Farmer A makes $100,000 profit per year. Farmer B makes $90,000 per year. On the whole they do almost equally well. Farmer A makes a little more but he works way harder than Farmer B. The real drawback for Farmer A is once in a while there is a mold that prevents the seed producers from producing seeds and sometimes this can last up to 2 or 3 seasons. Some seasons he can barely find any seeds at all. Sure, a few of his old plants do come back to life each year but not even a tenth as many as farmer B's plants do. But not Farmer B. He cares about his plants, not just their yields. In fact those plants are his friends. He goes out for a few hours each day and tends to them, even in colder months.

Back to reality, what have we learned? We're thinking about growing strong, healthy plants from seeds instead of just maximizing yields during harvest. The yields will take care of themselves. Look, 99% of all of you reading this book are starting a small business that you are hoping to become medium sized business some day. You are seriously fucking yourself trying to drum up new business all the time. Meanwhile you are getting perfectly good seeds strewn about and while you look for their fruits during harvest, you never pay them attention again. The plants wither away and you're left with depleted soil and a lot of work ahead of you.

So how does this tie in to business? We know that people love good customer service. They love it so much because it's rare. GREAT customer service is even more rare. The best? Well the best gets loyalty that other brands and companies never get. This is where your strengths should be focused once your product or service is mastered. Of course you will need a repeatable process for efficient order fulfillment but that's another book.

So what does the best customer service actually look like? How about a company that reaches out to you before you reach out to them with a problem? No, not a mass email. Actually reach out. Oh, you don't have time right? Ok so keep buying leads, paying for advertising and searching for new business. Don't forget that getting new business costs money, one way or the other. Until, that is, your engagement foundation has been laid and cemented on. You have sprouted enough seeds of genuine communications and connections. Then, everything starts to grow on its own. Oh yeah, I forgot the part where you showed the plants so much love, they not only keep growing back, but they plant seeds of their own and these plants, man these plants grow faster somehow. And if you take care of these too?!?! Well, then you've got yourself a farm that is ready to be tended to leisurely and pleasurably. The yields you get back will be plenty, and you'll discover a new meaning to life. Serving others. Being there for others. Earning their praise. Praise will energize the shit out of you. Do you know what it's like to get 5-10 emails a day telling you what an amazing job you are doing and how you are crushing it? Some will bring tears to your eyes, others joy to your heart, no bullshit. People will bring you into their lives, and you will enjoy the work you are putting into establishing a true foundation of community supporting your business!

And now you are entering a new place not many others in the business world have travelled to before.

Friendships. Your clients become your friends. You start really understanding them, becoming familiar with their lives and families, and even creating solutions to their problems. (In my case, my members' problems with cigar services were information and excitement related. They had no information on the products or people who made them. And there was zero excitement. More on that later.) My members and customers are truly my friends. I genuinely do feel this way 100%. The entire way through I would think to myself, this is a business, because it is, but these are NOT just sales. These are relationships that I am building through business. You want to know something else? I've discovered some amazing otherwise unheard of brands and business partners THROUGH my relationships with members. Why? Because the excitement for our brand is palpable and my members don't feel like customers, but rather members of a movement who want to share their own unique experiences with other members.

That's what is different about this style of business we call Communal Commerce. I'm pooling my money with my friends every month to go out and get us the best damn cigars on the planet. That's how I see it. Of course, I get paid for my time but that is the fee. That is included in the cost of goods. And I have the best job in the world! It's literally like being the beer run person at the party. Give me the money, I'll be back, except THIS beer run person aims to impress! How do we do this, you ask? Over time, you will develop your own style. But the basics are keeping a curious mind about your clients. WHO are THEY? Find out. Contact them. Ask them what they liked, what they didn't like, what they do for a living and everything else you may be curious about. Not through some piece of shit survey junk mail either. When you think about your available time, energy, and priorities as a business owner, you should be prioritizing these conversations as an essential part of your business strategy. It's not something to save for when there is free time. Keep up with your clientele!

Once a person is doing business with you, you can start learning from them. How can you keep their business? How can you turn a one time transaction into a longterm relationship? Start with this. Reach out and touch someone. This should be an email. Not a mass email. It could be a phone call, if this is a business that requires phone calls, but honestly, establishing communication through social media and or email is the only way to go long term these days. Now, did you reach out to them first? Awesome if so, but how far along in the process? I believe it should come a little up front, like, "How did you find out about me?"

Let's talk about the voice you're using in these emails, too. This is important. People want to talk to YOU. Not a faceless representative of your company. Remember when people believed there was power in words like "us," and "we," and other corporate lingo that created a false sense of friendly professionalism that nobody really bought to begin with? Like, "Hey John we have an idea for you!" or "We would like to know what you think!" WE is bullshit. I want to know who I'm actually speaking to, and I'm not going to genuinely engage with some corporate script. I actually care about John. So I make a little contact up front. And then a good, engaging follow up after the experience has been had. This is the best way to make your service or product better. Getting access to your clients' true feelings about said service or product will make you the best in what you do. So, even if you are not that curious about the actual person, you must be curious as to what product or service is getting the best and worst responses, right? This is where all the power a business owner has, comes from. And I bet 99% of all business owners don't give two fucks about this part. This is how you can get into a market and carve a new section of it out for yourself and people like you. My members are a lot like me. We have similar tastes and I can at least understand their taste if they are not the same as me. Who are your people? What made them come to you? Why are they, or are they not, coming back? Look, you spend a certain amount of money on a regular basis on leads and procuring new business every month, and every year. By nurturing the relationships that used to be clients into becoming more like friends, you will eventually be able to stop buying leads and paying for marketing. Your new friends will do it for you.

Now the next step. You already reached out and engaged your potential new friend. They got their order or service delivered and now it's time to reach out again. Let me tell you what NOT to do. Surveys, mass emails, and/or ask for reviews. Just ask them, friend to friend, how was the product/service? Use their name. In the beginning phases of growing your business, you should have plenty of time to do this. Make friends. I'm a person who has moved around a lot. My friends are few and far between. That is, until Privada Cigar Club. I have people who I consider friends, "sisters and brothers of the leaf" as we call one another, in every city and town across the country. The new world is an online one, and social media connections and email penpals are your new friends, like it or not. HOWEVER! It is important to keep in mind that while your follower count is visible, and easy to obsess over, it means nothing if these aren't leads you are following up on. Consider them human beings, and potential friends. Don't think of them as numbers. To give you an idea of what I mean, our typical YouTube videos get anywhere between 5,000-20,000 views, some closer to 50,000. While that's pretty high for the cigar industry, they are not much compared to popular YouTubers in other industries. But if you look closer at our engagement, you'll see that each video has hundreds, some thousands, of comments. That is what real engagement looks like. And guess what, they are engaged because we are all friends and we are a community.

Let's bring this back to your business. Engage. Here's another example. In real time, as I write this, I just bought watch modification parts on a site called DLW. Rolex pissed me off so bad I'm into customizing Seikos now. I made two purchases. I paid shipping on both orders. Before I could email the company to ask them to consolidate the order and possibly refund the shipping on one order, they did the refund and emailed me and told me they were doing so. Ready for this? The owner himself also emailed me with a concern about my order. Two parts I bought do not fit together. He wanted to make sure I understood this. I know his name now. I know he cares more about his customers' satisfaction than their money. I know he cares. I know he knows his stuff. This kind of makes him an authority, does it not? I'm his customer, after all. I'm coming to him. This puts him in a particular position. He is off to a great start, although missing a few key components that could potentially really put him over the top, which I will address later.

Take a moment to digest this information and think about how to organically engage people that buy your product or service. And the next time I need Seiko mod parts, guess who I will go to first?

Man I saw this email title and was expecting a link to a survey online or something and thought to myself I would love to take a survey for privada. But then I saw it's an email from Brian! To me that is why I am in this club. Your not just another number that gets a link to a survey your a human being that Brian welcomes into his family.

I have loved being in this club. I love how much I am learning. I learned I really like a thinner Guage lancero. And I have developed my tasting palate. I never used to get the nuances of the cigar like I did before. The community and fellowship because of this club and cigars in general this year has been great!

Now you ask how I'm doing and how's life. I am thankful for my provisions. I think that's the best way I can sum up this year. My mom and dad got covid but they are fine. I have had more volunteer work helping them and their business this year on top of my regular 9-5. Thankfully weekends I help my parents. But I am still thankful for good health. Me and my wife are healthy and she has actually gotten a promotion this year. I working from home struggle with finding motivation and miss the office some days but yet I am thankful I still have a job. On days I do manage to get a cigar in I always try to count my blessings. I'm 28 years old married, about to get a puppy, financially stable smoking cigars and enjoying the finer things in life. It can only get better from here!

Here's to you Brian and privada family!

Sam

"The more you engage with customers the clearer things become and the easier it is to determine what you should be doing."

John Russell

President, Harley Davidson

Chapter 3

Authoritize.

Put a Face on it and Teach

*B*efore we get into this section, let's address the elephant in the room. I'm aware that you won't find the word "Authoritize" in the dictionary. So I'm going to define it for you here: to Authoritize is to make yourself the authority on a given topic. It starts with a passion for something, then continues with becoming wholly educated on the topic and turns you into the figure of authority on that topic. Make sense? Cool. Let's keep it moving.

You started a business, so you must know something about your product or service. Maybe this means taking things to the next level, from a hobby to a passion, and dedicating some time to really learning the ins and outs of the industry. You need to be an authority on some level in this regard. The good news is that between YouTube and Google, you will find enough information on just about anything to make you knowledgable. Getting certified can help too. Talking to others in the business helps also, but do not let their negativity wear off on you. I guarantee you I could make myself a master baker by first reading books, second watching YouTube tutorials and third working in a bakery for 1 month for free (IF, and only if, I was actually able to work hands-on with the bakers themselves. Not all just grunt work.) The point is these are your avenues for learning. Books, the internet and working for someone else in the field. School too, but don't get caught up in this. I never worked for anyone else in my field. I didn't attend cigar university. I did read a lot and I most certainly practiced often and watched countless hours of YouTube videos from people who knew more than me. I like the subject, so it was fun. This business model grew for me organically out of my passion and my own networks. For me, it was about having fun, learning more about something I found deeply fascinating, and engaging with people I enjoyed communicating with. I did catch on to a few things that others who have way more experience than me in the field learned the tough way.

I have tasted a lot of cigars, and I've worked very intentionally on developing a nuanced palate. I'm one of those assholes who will tell you to look for notes of bittersweet cocoa and cayenne pepper in your cigar. I also did something else most others don't do in the cigar world, and that is tell you exactly what to pair each cigar with. I smoke the cigars I'm selling myself, and I write suggestions of both food and beverages that will enhance the smoking experience. There have been several instances when an idea for a pairing would come to mind and I would go out of my way to make that food myself or have my wife make it, or make that beverage/cocktail to experiment. Nine times out of ten it would be a hit. Who knew this would be a super power of mine and a huge part of the total Privada experience? Remember, there is only one you. YOU are what makes your company unique. You must be able to talk shop with other authorities in your field, but then you must also figure out what you uniquely bring to the table that others do not.

Another thing I brought to the table was approachability, youth, and down-to-earth coolness. I was used to old school cigar guys. A little bit pretentious, usually over the age of 65, living at his local brick and mortar shop intimidating the hell out of newbies and casual smokers. So I was the opposite of my predecessors. I'm a millennial, I have good taste, I put an effort into my appearance and self-presentation, and I keep things friendly and completely unpretentious! I started making approachable content that could appeal to both seasoned smokers and newbies. I put my face on it and I did it with style! Write that down too.

Be the opposite of what people are used to, and tired of, in your industry.

Everyone treating your product like a commodity? Do the opposite. Treat it like art. Everyone leaving out information and not explaining the process? Do the opposite. Be completely transparent. Document every part of the process and SHARE it. Maybe that means you start a YouTube channel or a simple blog site. Bring your personality and super powers to the table, do the opposite of what others are doing and KNOW as much, or more, than most in your field. That, my friends, is a recipe for success.

Let's put this into real-world terms with a good example. I don't want you thinking that you have to be a horologist just to sell watches or even watch parts. This is important. I never rolled a cigar. I have never farmed tobacco. I don't know the first thing about either of those topics. I do know, however, why one brand's tobacco tastes different from others. I understand what a good Broadleaf wrapper tastes like versus a San Andres leaf wrapper, and I know where they come from. I know how to taste and then review a cigar, and I have read about all the different tobacco leaves. I know about the major farms and I can taste the difference between their products. Nonetheless, I guarantee you the people who came before me think I'm a fucking poser. It's not important as long as I know what I'm talking about in regards to the end product. What flavors to look for.

A food critic does not have to be able to cook the food. A food critic understands how flavors in food work together and what good food tastes like. And it works in the opposite manner as well. Find your niche, and develop your knowledge and expertise there. Ignore the haters. There are very few farmers in our industry that have the imagination and have read enough cigar reviews to pick out the flavors that I get when smoking a cigar. And I also want to say that this information I have learned, studied, and practiced, did not all come to me by magic in the beginning. I did not know much more than how to taste a cigar and what to pair it with. And those things are subjective.

So yeah, I bet a lot of the old school guys in my business, the ones who treated this like a commodity, think that dissecting the flavors of a cigar is a pointless endeavor for dorks. Maybe they do not respect me. I've made them even more mad by going on to create new, more modern ways of thinking about cigar culture, and even reviving some old school ways of doing simple things. Like lighting a cigar. Like aging cigars. Like cutting and smoking cigars. All complete with my own uniquely adapted traditional verbiage and variations of old techniques.

So please, know that if you do this right, other people who are senior to you are going to talk shit. One guy even told me that I'm just making things up.

Making things up is called creation, invention, or idealism. It is perfectly acceptable to consider this practice if what you are talking about is true and can be seen as true. For instance, cigars need to rest after they are made. Depending on the leaf, most manufacturers will not allow the cigars to be shipped without spending at least 90 days in the aging rooms. But, most of the people before me were selling a commodity. So, you can imagine, when demand goes up, that 90 days goes out the window and it's time to make money. Those cigars are what we call in the box, wet. Most home enthusiasts are obsessed with humidity. Most people over-humidify in my opinion. Regardless, when a cigar is wet it smokes poorly. I teach my people to look for signs of wetness and if found, ready for this, "dry age" or "dry box" the cigars for a few hours to a few days so that they lose extra humidity. I don't believe I made that term up, but I most certainly made it popular among my people. This is what prompted that veteran of our industry (For whom I have nothing but respect) to say I make things up. "Dry boxing, what the fuck is that? You just let it dry out kid!" That's the kind of thing I'm talking about. Now, when people think of the term "dry boxing" that have seen my YouTube video on dry boxing, they think of me and subsequently, Privada too.

Looking at something like this as just an example, it is a fantastic opportunity for you to create content and social media buzz around your business! Educate your people. Answer their questions. Give them new avenues to explore, give them new vocabularies, and engage them in a conversation! If there's a question that comes up multiple times in multiple conversations, make a video or a post about it, in addition to answering these questions one-on-one! Social media is a good tool to use for this, but don't let it stop there.

I believe that naïveté or freshness or youthfulness in the industry made me 100% a better teacher or communicator of information because I am excited about what I just learned. And I know how to explain it to a beginner. A veteran knows so much he's forgotten more than you know and is far from excited about what he knows. For me there is nothing better than discovering something about my craft and directly passing that information on to my people. How we do that is another book! But again, it's not through mass email. Stop sending me fucking impersonal mass emails!

So learn everything you can about your product or service and pass that information along to your friends. IF you have passion for what you are doing, or at least the result you are getting, this should be fun.

From: ▮▮▮▮▮▮▮▮▮▮

Date: *February 6, 2021 at 4:49:21 PM EST*
To: *info@privadacigarclub.com*
Subject: This last year...

☐ *Hey Brian,*

I'm not usually one to get all sappy about stuff, but today is my 50th birthday and I just wanted to take a moment to truly thank you and tell you how much this club means to me. My wife got me my membership for my birthday last year, and I was just thinking about what an incredible journey the past year has been.

I used to get cigars once in a while at my local shop, but I didn't really know much about them and couldn't tell anything from comparing flavors let alone pairings! It was a special occasion kind of thing. Then, Privada came into the picture. Between your tasting and pairing notes, the youtube stuff, and the incredible sticks I've been getting every month, not to mention all the help you've given me personally along the way any time I asked, cigars have really become a huge part of my life.

Since covid hit I started truly diving into the experience and even started my own cigar log. I've learned so much about how the wrapper, construction, and factory can affect my experience and I feel like I'm part of something "bigger."

I've learned how to store my cigars properly and I've learned how to tell the difference between actual quality and hype. When my wife makes something good for dinner I immediately know what I want to pair with it. I feel like I'm in the Know. So thank you Brian. This year has been so amazing even though the world is crazy, and Privada has made all the difference. #weareprivada truly!

Kyle

"Knowledge is power."

Francis Bacon

Attorney General, Lord Chancellor of England, 1561

Chapter 4

Engage. Foster Community

Let's say there's something to celebrate coming up, and all your friends are in town, and everyone is excited about getting together. Perfect recipe for a party! A get together. This is the kind of atmosphere and energy you are building when it comes to the engagement of your business. You've already gotten them to engage with YOU, now, is it possible to get them to engage with each other? I'm personally a firm believer that if you have a group of people that all agree on something, there is a synergy that gets created. It's something special. Others take notice too. Think QAnon, think Wall Street Bets. And like a wave, the momentum will grow and the tide will surge! You are creating a movement. That is, if you have properly served, engaged, and encouraged your people. Of course, you will have to be exciting people all along the way, but it's not as hard as it seems, and we will get back to that shortly. You can theorize or learn different ways to do this through other examples and or teachings. But, I have to tell you something. Of all the pieces of this puzzle, this is, somehow, simultaneously the most, and the least important part. Most businesses do not require you to build a dedicated and loyal community to build a solid six-figure company, but if you can, this is where you can go from small to middle/large scale with tools you have at your disposal right now.

CAUTION. You may not want to get there. If you simply want to make a good living without too much stress, and nothing MORE, there is no need. The stress of a multi-million dollar company can tip scales, and it isn't necessarily for everyone. But even if it's on a small scale, if you find that you can create community around your business, do it! It works and it will tip the scales in favor of your business's momentum and lead to tons of success.

So, building community. You want to do it, now how do you start? Let's think a bit about how groups of human beings work. What makes them tick? What motivates them, sparks desire or inspires frustration? What causes people to unite and support something? In some old fashioned, deeply rooted, primordial way, gangs are cool. Of course not the violence that's associated with it. What I'm talking about is more of the aesthetic side of things, and the group dynamic. The jackets, the patches and the colors. It signifies unity and togetherness. We know they are wrong, but gangs have existed since the beginning of the human race and continue to remain now.

So how do we offer the opportunity to join a gang, you might ask? How can we cultivate our business into the group dynamic? Being a part of something is a very powerful feeling. And we don't always call them gangs anymore, either. Some of our country's most intelligent people join legal gangs like political parties, clubs, college fraternities/sororities, secret societies, etc. Group validation around a common belief is a powerful thing.

I am a person who never truly subscribed to joining other peoples' causes. I always had my own, or thought I was too cool to be a part of someone else's movement. I missed out. I missed out on easy access to friends and good times. I would have never joined a cigar club, and look at all the amazing things I would have missed out on. Most people don't share my loner tendencies. Most people innately understand the benefits of being part of a group. There is sharing, not only of goods, but of knowledge, access to things, and energy. We all want what we want and we don't want to have to work too hard for it. Groups. Gangs. Clubs…they all allow us access to things we could not have had access to on our own, and definitely not as quickly.

First things first, what are you offering your potential gang members? There needs to be a clear benefit as to why they are a part of the movement in the first place. In my case, it is access to rare cigars they cannot find elsewhere. Even more so, each cigar comes with a write up, tasting notes and pairing notes. No one else did that before Privada, either. So the value is there. I serve my people better than anyone else out there.

That's the reason they join the movement.

Now, think about how much fun it is to talk about your favorite pizza or sushi place with other people who have eaten there also. You are in line at the bank or grocery store somewhere, and bored out of your mind, you start talking to someone. They say they are from Small Townsville, and you're like, "Smalltownsville! I go there all the time! Ever been to Seito, the sushi joint?" And they respond with something like, "Yes of course I love that place. The guy that opened that place is my friend's sister's cousin!" People WANT to talk about the things they experience! Surprise! There is your marketing strategy. Just make sure they have GOOD things to say to each other.

Fucking Yelp! They built an EVIL empire based off this kind of thing, man. They channeled the desire to share experiences, and now it can make or break a business before their next customer even bothers to walk in the door. People listen to each other. They listen to the reviews. And they *share*.

The same goes for social media. The gang effect. You have to make sure the positive things stand out, and your people will talk! You follow Privada Cigar

Club. Years ago, a member began using the hashtag #weareprivada that you've now already subscribed to and followed. He posts a picture of a cigar you smoked last night and fell in love with. You comment that it was amazing, he writes back, "Thanks I loved it too." Next post you make, he comments on. And so a friendship ensues. Normally, this would not lead to real friendship but because you are both *club members* who have an obvious shared interest and get similar experiences each month, you now share something bigger than just liking a picture.

You will soon hear the word *club* being thrown around a lot in larger businesses. Customer service titles will go away. Club member services will appear. Communal Commerce will rear its head in to corporate America. The beauty of communal commerce is that it is so easy to spot authenticity through it so the fakers will get weeded out fast! But customer service will never be the same.

Now, when you engage in relationship building exercises often, you can not only build the bridge between you and the member or client, but they will begin to engage between and amongst themselves as well. Contests are great for this. Events are great for this. Events can feel a little corny, especially in the FOMO-fueled social media world of the online recluse. I have no idea how the events of 2020 will change and reshape social interaction in the future, but it's hard to imagine going fully back to the way things were, and at this point it doesn't matter. Speculation is pointless. Either way, the concept of creating excitement is the same online or in person. Get your people talking. This can backfire on you at times, because if, for example, two people post about bad construction on a cigar in one day, the people that are following don't necessarily see the 9,998 other people who loved it. In that day, those two problematic products were on display and at least some of the people will be left with that image In their minds. Also, be prepared for the fact that you will lose groups of people at times. They may not like the newer members, or they may remember when it was just you and the product was a certain way. This is all part of growing. If you have a small business, and keep it small, this may never happen to you. But be prepared for the fact that some people will grow out of the group. Be on the lookout for toxic people constantly.

Toxic people bring negativity to the table. Fuck them! If you see them, cut them off at the head ASAP. If you let them slide, eventually you will be left with a group of negative, nasty people who make others feel stupid for asking questions. Tend to your community and make sure things are welcoming. POSITIVITY rules the day in group building.

Let's think of this from a regular business point of view. I'll give you an example. Okay, let's say you you sell appliances. I recently bought a Viking oven. It's the high end of the mid-grade appliances. Some would argue it is high end period, but the cost was about $4,500 and there are other products for this size that go up to $9,000. A regular oven costs as low as $800. The point is, this is the Range Rover of ovens. As someone who never bought a Viking product before, I expected my experience to be different than buying any old oven from Scratch and Dent World. It was not. In fact, it was worse. Way worse.

(Speaking of disappointing experiences, I bought a few Rolexes in the past few years. One was $40,000. In my mind, a watch with that kind of price tag would have come with a full experience of a private room, white gloved fitting, bottles of champagne, all the pomp and circumstance, ego boosting compliments lavished upon me, followed by access to other, more exclusive products.. Honestly, these hopes were dashed! They took my credit card, sold me a watch and offered me sparkling water. It was a tepid reception for such a prestigious luxury purchase).

But let's focus on the appliances first. I promise these stories have a point! The bad experience really started for me when I had to follow up with my sales representative. BAD. My sales rep also gave me a vibe I didn't like. Something along the lines of, "Everyone wants a Viking, but few follow through, so I'm going to send you the paper work, and after I see you have signed it and paid, I'll get back with you." Right off the bat, BAD. If you want to wait until a purchase is made, I understand… sort of. Maybe if that's the gatekeeping experience, and it eventually leads to something spectacular. Maybe it could build hype or give an illusion of exclusivity. But no, not for this customer. And again, after the purchase was made, I received no follow up. BAD. The products were delivered weeks later missing a vital piece. BAD! You get it. This is subpar but standard or typical practice in American business. It's all kinds of missteps like these. Put your money down, they get you your product, you go home. Standard. BASIC! It doesn't sit right with me as a consumer, or a business owner, so I did something about it.

Okay, here is how this Viking oven purchase looks with a Communal Commerce approach. I'm spitballing here. We will pretend I own an appliance store and am an authorized Viking dealer. Let's say a customer calls in to inquire about a product. Me, or my sales rep have a bullet point list of 3-4 things we say on each call that we know make people feel good about the experience. We make sure we take note of their name and ask them plenty of questions during this initial contact. Questions like: Why did you choose this oven in particular (Maybe I can sell you a more expensive model, or maybe you don't need such an expensive one?)

Are you remodeling your kitchen? Your home? Do you maybe even have more than one home? Does your family cook a lot? You get the point. I would probably schedule an appointment to go see the kitchen space, but for the sake of saving time and money if we cannot do that until deposits are made, fine. I do request a video of the kitchen by email or maybe even FaceTime. In the real scenario, my sales rep did request a video, but only to see the current model I had. I would want the entire space so I can build a rapport and maybe up-sell or recommend other products the client may not know about. That said, after I give the person the info, I look to make some personal connection with why they are buying this product. The guy's wife is turning 35, she's a home chef and she always dreamed of owning a Viking. Team Viking to the rescue! You figure out what model works for them, and your potential customer does not bat an eye at the price. He wants to make sure his wife is getting the best, and he is ready to join team Viking. If he doesn't pay then, I shoot him an email tomorrow confirming the conversation. Once a payment is made, the experience begins.

Let's bear in mind, this can be tough in situations where the product will take 30-60 days to arrive, but once the commitment is there, we follow up once per week or every other week letting them know things are on schedule. Remember, I'm just continuing to spitball some ideas on how Communal Commerce would shake things up.

My appliance store has a Facebook group, Instagram page or my own social networking technology or forum that I add them to. I also get them to subscribe to my YouTube channel, where I have online tutorials on each product I sell, plus videos on how to make certain things with the product. Maybe I even send branded accessories confirming the purchase and creating loyalty. Here is where we really get different. The other appliance store town that is an authorized Viking dealer just sells you the product. Our products come with a free monthly in-person or online cooking class. It's in real time. Not a YouTube video, but maybe a YouTube live streaming event. All the people who bought that product recently get the first $350.00 course for free. We even have local chefs or businesses like Williams Sonoma who donate their time because we expose them to clients in their demographic. So, now we offer more value than anyone else who sells our product. Starting to see the picture?

But here is the kicker. During the class we partner people up. We introduce ourselves and engage with the clients and encourage them to engage with each other…anyone want wine? Hell, my class might even be held at a hot restaurant in town. You'd be surprised the kind of partnerships you can make with other businesses once the momentum is going and things are mutually beneficial! "Hey Chef, I've got a group of 5-10 people who care so much about food they are willing to spend 10 times more on an oven. Think it would be good to meet these people in person and tell them why they should eat at your place more often?"

You see where this is going. But it's not over there. Once I've got them learning about their craft, their new product, and adding to their skill base (in other words, *serving* my clients), I pick one or two that are charismatic and I ask them to join me on our YouTube page for a tutorial. I shoot a video— good, bad, or ugly, this video will work. If you have an iPhone or a cheap DSLR camera, you can make this work. You can also hire people who normally shoot weddings or family photos and guarantee them work each month for a major price break, etc. Video has become a lot easier and I have to stress, it doesn't have to look amazing. The content of the videos is what matters .

Now we have Donna, she's using her new Viking Model XYZ and she's going to make a casserole with us today. We make Donna look awesome through the power of editing. Then we send this to our clients' phones along with an invite to our happy hour, or cooking class, or online Zoom call about how your experience with your oven has been, and what you could be doing better or might be doing wrong etc. We are creating a whole world for them to enter now that they are the proud owners of a new Viking! They're not going to get bored and forget about this hobby. They're going to stay EXCITED!

Now, I understand that this requires extra work and a little bit of money. But here's the deal. My competitor just took out an advertisement for $1,800 in some local newspaper or magazine that no one reads. I spent $600. My competitor is going to get a few one off sales and squander them, like what happened with me when I received a lukewarm welcome with no follow up. Or worse yet, I'll give them negative advertising like I did and will continue to do with the company I purchased from. That means, not only no repeat business, but I'm going to urge my friends to stay away from this bad company. Oh boy. So now they have to spend $1,800 per month just doing damage control, which goes up in cost every year and is an expense, not an investment. They also have no clue if it will keep working. This is palliative care for a business with a prognosis. Why not focus on keeping the business healthy? Some of the customers they do get will become negative advertisers or just one-time customers. This can force them to have to spend even more in ad dollars. They will send out mass emails and hope that they can get 2% response on them. For those of you not familiar with mass email marketing, 2% is actually good advertising returns in most business. And the worst part, each month, day, week, they start over. Hoping the market will still have a demand for their product and hoping their ad will capture a little sliver of that market.

I'm going to explain this next part briefly. I believe in abundance. Most entrepreneurs believe in the opposite, that there is a finite amount of business to be had in their industry. There is a false sense of scarcity. Let's think about the classic pie metaphor. If someone else in that industry is doing business they are taking a big old slice from that pie. This means less business pie slice for our entrepreneur, the way he sees things. Untrue. The more the competition gets business, the more you lose. Untrue. I do not subscribe to this way of thinking. Here is why. This isn't a pie. This is more like a farm. The more work and momentum in the field, the more it grows. Communal Commerce CREATES CUSTOMERS. Communal Commerce brings in new customers to your market. Communal commerce means investing in growth, not damage control.

When the 2020 pandemic hit the world, just about every industry was impacted, premium cigars included. Brick and mortar shops found themselves either locked down or severely lacking customers. As an online retailer, we were not badly affected, but I saw what was happening to cigar culture as brick and mortar retailers were hurting. The instincts of most entrepreneurs in my position would be to say "Awesome! Screw the in person shops and let's focus on growing our online shop". While we did some of that, we also looked to lend a helping hand to brick and mortar retailers by starting what we called the Limited Cigar Association. We used our marketing prowess to start a network of a few hundred shops across the United States, provide them limited quantities of one highly sought after cigar each month and then send our members to these stores to share in the excitement. It was and continues to be, a phenomenon that the industry has never before seen. Most shops sell out of the stock within hours. Shops are seeing foot traffic increases in the double digits and our members are finding shops in their area they never knew existed. We didn't have to do this. We didn't have to share our audience with brick and mortar shops. We lent them our COMMUNITY, something most entrepreneurs would NEVER do. Turns out, our members spent a lot more money than I expected when visiting these shops. But in the end, we served not only our members but our industry (which is a form *back serving*). If what you do is truly good for the movement, not just yourself and it serves your community, you will not go wrong.

Let me explain further with the oven buying example. By the way, one thing I have to mention is that half of my friends in my cigar club barely bought cigars before they found Privada. The experience I created for them along with the engagement, excitement, and community I paired them with made them want to get into cigars more.

So Donna does our cooking tutorial. By the way, Donna is an attorney who was in a local magazine recently in one of those "who's who about town" gossip columns in her local area...not bad, right! A couple of the other wives of the schmucks that pay 10 times what you should for an oven read that magazine. It tickled them to be a part of this class with Donna. It lets them know they are in good company. And even if Donna was not some local superstar, but was just charismatic and funny, or easy to watch, they still feel warm about getting out there, socializing and most importantly, learning how to be the best at-home chef. Well, Tom, Dave, Alice, Fernanda and Mercedes are all viewers of the class too. Tom is a gay man who is known in the LGBTQ community and has an amazing social network locally. Mercedes is married to the new point guard for the local basketball team. Fernanda's a stay-at-home mom and the PTA president. Dave is a douche (hey, I'm trying to be realistic here, not everyone is going to be all sunshine, rainbows, and valuable connections, but we still have to deal with them) and Alice is local interior designer. These people all know people. Lots of people. They want to show off their skills when people come around. As cooking shows get bigger and these folks flex on guests with amazing recipes, INTEREST gets created. Eventually the conversation becomes, "What oven you are using?" Their guests say things like, "I wish I could get into cooking!" And, as they become exposed to these local community influencers who are becoming friends through your cooking expos, they start to invite their other friends to the expos and talk to these friends, exposing them to the things they learned from you. And if you are halfway decent at this, they talk about you, your business and the value they took from you serving them and making them a part of your community of burgeoning at-home chefs.

Some of you entrepreneurs were so intuitive you created badges, patches, gifs, hashtags, aprons (DOPE APRONS), spatulas, bakeware etc., the list goes on. These are small investments, but these things are visible in-person and online and act as a calling card for your business. You collaborated with local makers and designers, and now your brand is making waves in THEIR circles. They all point back to you.

Now some of Mercedes' friends, the athlete wives, are going to re-do their kitchens. Mercedes is not letting them shop at Best Buy. They go to you. Same thing with the rest of them. By year two, your parties are more frequent and much more exciting. By now, your old clients are so jealous with excitement that they want new appliances. Hey, I used to love Rolex, but I just saw an AP Royal Oak that I want now, too. Now it's the stove range, or the microwave. Hell, you're so hot right now you are thinking about creating your own line of appliances and branching out from the Viking franchise. Word is out, cooking at home is for ballers, baller's wives, heads of the PTA, and the like. And if you aren't using a Viking, you're not cooking. And if you didn't get that Viking from YOU then you fucked up. WOW. Communal Commerce. Oh and…your Instagram is popping! The Facebook group is nuts. People tag you every day with pictures of their new recipes. And you spend time on this. Replying to them. Letting them know how proud you are of them. How far they've come or how good they are at this. And how LUCKY you are to have them in your community.

THIS is Community. This is communal

commerce. And once you have a community, it's time to EXCITE!

From: █████████

Date: Thu, Dec 31, 2020 at 9:48 PM

Subject: Re: So....

To: <info@privadacigarclub.com>

Brian,

Just left Selwood Cigars here in Portland, Oregon.(LCA Shop here in P-Town)

I grabbed a 5 pack of the Thai Tea - Looking forward to smoking one tonight.

I was also fortunate enough to find/purchase a full box of Robert Caldwells "Hand Signed" 2020 Limited Release, Eastern Standard Sungrown, Magic Super Lancero (Box 314 of 1000).

Nothing would make me happier than sharing a great meal, some Cognac and burning a stick with you two. Only way to make it better would be for Matt Booth and Clark to join the three of us...

I can't seem to get enough of your guy's antics on YouTube - My Girlfriend thinks I'm nuts watching all your videos and interviews. Each of them has been particularly helpful and enjoyable as I journey back into the world of Cigars. The industry and quality of today's smokes are so much better than they were in the late 90's when I first started smoking. The passion and education Espinosa, Booth, Perdomo, Caldwell and yourself bring to today's consumers is truly appreciated and remarkable.

Thank you for that...

In all honesty, I've enjoyed all the smokes you've sent. Some more than others, but I have yet to snub one out mid smoke unpleased.

I've been super impressed and have really enjoyed the Farm Rolled cigars as well. I actually had my doubts about that portion of the program but it was quickly washed away after diving into the first batch I received.

Not to get all mushy on you... but your Privada cigar program, passion and videos have become the way I decompress from an otherwise Pressure Cooker of a career/job.

Today, my team of professional homebuilders closed our 450th new house in Fiscal Year 2020. Many of the members of my leadership team have worked alongside me for 10 to 20 years. Recently, several of them have been joining me for an after work cigar and adult beverage to shake off the stress of the day/week. They too are becoming a part of our cigar story and journey... Thank you for that.

Looking forward to receiving my December Box and Farm Rolled bag...

Be well - Stay Healthy - Stay Safe
All my best to you, your family and Privada in 2021
Happy New Year!

Appreciative,
Dave

"*There is no power for change greater than a community discovering what it cares about.*"

Margaret J. Wheatley

American Writer and Management Expert who studies
organizational behavior

Chapter 5

Excite. Don't Sleep

This is where you can really have a lot of fun. I understand that not all of us are super creative, but all of us can create excitement within our customer base. Like I previously mentioned, if it's exciting to you, it will excite them, too. Keep things fresh and collaborate frequently. All businesses spend money on marketing, whether it ends up being through buying leads, advertising or referral fees. The Communal Commerce business model is set up so that at some point, you will not need to purchase leads or pay for marketing. This means about 15-30% more profits. This means you can do less business than your competition and still make more money. This also leaves you a lot more time and resources to focus on step 1, serving. This means you can INVEST in improving your client's experience instead of spending needlessly on damage control to prop up a subpar product!

Who's better than you, huh? You laid your foundation properly. You served your client base like no other and added value to their lives. You engaged them, creating not just a business rapport, but friendships. You've made such an impression that your customers won't want to shop anywhere else in your industry. You also encouraged them to engage communally, turning your new friends and clients into their new friends, thus creating a community. They're doing the job of advertising for you, and it's worth about a thousand times more than some sponsored post or in-print ad.

Three major pillars are out of the way. You've made the shift to Communal Commerce , and it's paying off big time. You've done your footwork and you've established something. This is where we excite your people. We keep the momentum going. We get to trigger more frequent and engaged online interaction amongst our community members through various campaigns. These can be simple, or super creative! I think it all starts with the giveaway. This is a great way to turn a like or a follow into REAL LIFE engagement. These people may or may not know each other, but you got them involved in your EXPERIENCE and now they get to share that experience with others who have had the same experience.

People want to share their experiences. People also want to be validated in their opinion of the experience. Let's scoop out a fresh example. I can give you the best ice cream in the world one time, and no one else will ever have it. You will never be able to discuss it with anyone because they cannot get it. We need to be able to share our experiences! Humans seek consensual validation with other humans, if you're into thinking like a psychologist.

Or, you eat at my ice cream parlor and it's the best ice cream ever. I also give you an address for an Instagram giveaway. Each week I pick a winner. Your entire family, up to 5 people, eat ice cream for free each week when you win. It's free to enter if you follow me on Instagram. So you're scrolling through Instagram, and you see the giveaway notice. It's a picture of the same ice cream you have been craving all week. You and 300 other locals "oooh" and "ahhh" over the picture in comments. Someone comments with a funny reaction gif. Others like the comment and post replies. I work my giveaway magic and reply to comments and tag others, thus encouraging engagement amongst the members participating in the thread. We just validated their excitement for our product or service. Validation is huge! Each week this happens. This is where you can convert the energy of social media into REAL community. Create a link between online engagement and real life. Your followers become customers and they start to know each other's handles and usernames. Then I host ice cream parties at a specific time in a specific place. Now people are starting to become friends through this ice cream place, and man! My only ad cost is giving away free ice cream once a week! Are you kidding me? Excite your people! Now everyone is addicted to my ice cream because it is the best. Because I gave them better service and because I engaged them online to find out who they really are and became friends with them. Now I've got them engagement amongst themselves finding social connections through my ice cream experience and finally they're part of my ice cream fan club, singing my praises to anyone who ever mentions ice cream to them. At this point. I don't have to give anything away, but I still do for the excitement. I also have pop up shops in different locations to keep it exciting. Every Friday I go to a different location. I put up a post showing where I am one hour prior and I only stick around that location for one hour so if you miss me you can still come by the shop, but if you show up you're going to see a bunch of people who validate your love for my ice cream, some of whom are actually becoming your friends around town.

Oh, but one day I get this idea to use food coloring in my ice cream. It's black. My cones are gold. Later I'm doing a one time special at the local Tiffany dealer with Tiffany blue colored ice cream. If Tiffany doesn't like it, we can work with the florist down the street. Edible floral ice cream cone arrangements. Find your people! Create partnerships! EXCITE!

This part is crucial: When thinking of ways to excite people, you have to think about what would excite you.

What kind of giveaway or product or service

would excite you enough to engage? I mean you have to have some interest in your own business, right? You had to have at least liked ice cream to get into making ice cream. Look at other ice cream places world wide. Look to Tokyo. Look to London. Look to Dubai. What are they doing? What can you do to be similar but put your own spin on? Black ice cream is nothing new, but I've never seen it on a cone dipped in gold sprinkles etc.

What would get you excited? How old are your typical customers? Mine are about 25-55. Most of us grew up on Sesame Street. If there is one thing I learned from Donald Trump's Make America Great Again campaign, it's that NOSTALGIA is one of the most powerful emotions. I released a cigar that had a band on it that looked like the Cookie Monster. The entire cigar social media world went nuts. We broke the internet. The cigar-obsessed corner of a very specific niche market internet community, anyway. This is the kind of energy you can channel.

And that's the thing. Are you creating excitement on your platform? In most businesses, aside from utilities, your customers have a choice. If you show them the Communal Commerce way, they will choose you more often than not. Your personality has to come out in your business. You have to give the people reasons to choose or not to choose you. I am sorry to mention Trump yet again but who is more polarizing? Businesses that took aim at him decided who their client base or friends were. Same thing for the businesses that supported him. You cannot have them all, typically. Maybe this is a bad example. I do not talk politics. Let alone side my business with Democrat or Republican parties. But I'm making a point. When you start clocking big numbers, you start becoming less and less afraid to lose business. You start being less afraid to show who you are as a company and as a person.

Here's a good example: LGBTQ ice cream. It exists— ever heard of Boy Gay Ice Cream in New York? It's a rainbow of colorful products sold through an ice cream shop that supports its community. They have a cone called the Salty Pimp and pictures of the Golden Girls on the walls. They choose right up front who is, and who is not, going to eat there, and I respect that, but more importantly, it triggers people who are in that community to go there, and to feel loyalty to the company from the get go. I think you can pick up what

I'm putting down, friends! Find your niche and leverage that potential!

If I'm going through Google listings, why would I choose you? Excitement is not just the final step in Communal Commerce, it's the first impression, too. And the best, cheapest, form of procurement of new customers. So you served your people. Engaged them. Got them to engage amongst each other. Excited them. And now they are hooked. This energy is contagious. This energy is what creates movements. People experiencing together, engaging each other, and creating community around your business. Communal Commerce creates movements. Now people are driving from the next town over for our pop-up shop ice cream. You can create urgency with different variations of excitement but that is another book. Eventually if you keep going, people are driving from the next county over. Until eventually, you have not had ice cream until you have had THIS ice cream. That's the movement.

As a fellow business owner, I task you with entertaining your customer base. In life, we have no idea what we are doing here or why. We need entertainment to pass the time without pondering life's meaning too much. Help your people do this. Give them something to enjoy! You can excite individually too. The best is to engage and excite at the same time. Take your top 10 friends and give them samples of experiments or new products. Things that you want their opinion on. Let them guide your decisions! LISTEN to them! Talk about building friendship!

From: ████████████

Date: Sun, Aug 16, 2020 at 3:40 PM

Subject: Cigar meditation

To: <info@privadacigarclub.com>

Hey Brian.

Just wanted to fire off a quick email just to say thanks for everything you do to make privada the best cigar club going. Im an EMT in the UK and have been in the trenches fighting against covid. Its been a rough few months dealing with this virus. And I think one of the best things that has helped me get through this is coming home after a 12 hour shift and lighting up a premium cigar and pouring myself a glass of whiskey just unwind, and put the day/night behind me. I have just finished smoking the Montenegro (amazing stick by the way!!!) while listening to your meditation on sound cloud and just wanted to say it was really enjoyable.

Definitely added to the smoking and relaxation experience. Looking forward any upcoming episodes. Keep up the amazing work.

#weareprivada

Peace

Mark

"People think of loyalty as a customer for a lifetime, but it's really much simpler than that. It's about the next time, every time."

Shep Hyken

Customer Service Expert, New York Times and Wall Street Journal Best Selling Author

Chapter 6

Repeat

Serve. Engage. Make yourself the authority. Encourage your people to engage amongst themselves. Excite them enough to want to do it again. Keep doing it. Daily, weekly, monthly or annually. Whichever most applies to your business and the amount of business you want to do. Make this as much of a priority as you would other essential parts of your business plan. Make a system for keeping track of things. I don't care if it's an old notebook and your favorite pen, or a perfectly organized and color-coded spreadsheet. Be consistent. If you're not good at keeping track of things, hire someone to do it for you. Prioritize the information and feedback your customers are giving you! I have to stress this too. Being genuine is so important. Keep it real. People see through an act. If you do not enjoy it, they probably won't either. If it does not excite you, it will not excite them. If you do not want to repeat the cycle again, they will not either. So hire people who enjoy it too! Keep your employees happy, treat them well, train them to care about the work, And do it all over again. Serve your people the best product at the right price and like no one has served them before. Engage with them personally and make them a part of your life genuinely. Encourage them to engage with each other and create community. Excite them with more product or options to keep their attention. Entertain them and they will want to do this again with you. That simple.

Once you have found a rhythm that works for you and your business has gone through several successful cycles of the Communal Commerce model, you can establish ways to keep the conversations going, check in with your people, and make room for the changes that are coming to fruition from their suggestions!

As the business grows, certain parts of your operation may be automated (NOT your contact with your clientele!) While it is a separate conversation from the Communal Commerce model, and a parallel conversation to automation, an important concept to keep in mind as a business owner is passive income. This is the first step in going from a small to medium sized business, and it is the first step to true financial independence.

Once your community grows and demand for your product or service keeps increasing, you'll need to figure out which aspects of the process can be streamlined and automated! Think about your order fulfillment process. Think about your appointment booking system. Think about the extra time you're spending in low-impact areas that could be transferred into more crucial areas of the business.

From: ████████

Date: Fri, Jan 15, 2021 at 3:12 AM

Subject: Re: Order 1013425

To: Privada Cigar Club <*info@privadacigarclub.com*>

Hello,

I just wanted to say thank you for the quick response of your team and the quick shipment of the cigars. I am a paramedic in California and I just got to say how much I appreciate a great cigar every now and again and your team delivered no pun intended. The care taken in the packaging and selection of the cigars was phenomenal and the addition of the Boveda pack was much appreciated. I can tell the pride you and your company takes in delivery and care of the product. Thank you so very much definitely made my night and many more to come.

Sincerely,

Jon EMT-P

"We are what we
repeatedly do.
Excellence, then, is not
an act, but a habit."

Aristotle

Chapter 7

Expand

So you started an appliance shop. You employed SEEE. It worked. You have repeated the process and found employees or partners who employ it with you and for you. Business is booming. The operation is expanding. You have more time to focus on intentionally growing your business and creating new ways to keep your customers' attention. One of the ways I expanded Privada Cigar Club was to reward my members by implementing their suggestions. The true beauty of Communal Commerce is the constant feedback loop. Always feel out what products are most exciting and really seek out what your people truly want. I understand my market's wants and needs better than any 20 year veteran out there. I'm in this business for 3 years, and I understand more than they do about what the consumer wants? How did they let that happen? I asked the members (not in a mass email), aside from the $26 per month you spend here, how much more money do you spend on cigars. I was astonished. I was leaving so much opportunity to serve my people on the table. Instead they were giving their money away to people who bastardize cigars and cigar culture. Fuck that!

Anyway, something had to be done. And it is not all about making money. It's about serving a community. The profit will come. So I created a program that allowed them to buy their less rare, daily cigars through me in an inexpensive way that did not cheapen the reputations of the cigar brands. In this case, it was taking the bands off the cigars and focusing on the factories. Sort of a wholesale direct type thing. It's called Farm Rolled. It is truly the best cigars in the industry being sold to the consumer directly from the factories. Cutting out the middle man, hence saving us all money. This is how I expanded Privada Cigar Club from a limited, private club into two subscription services that catered to two different needs of the cigar community as well as an online shop with hundreds of offerings.

But what about our kitchen appliance entrepreneur? Or our smash hit ice cream parlor popup? It all comes down to the needs and wants of the people. Listen to their wildest dreams about your company's trajectory and offerings. If something isn't feasible just yet, don't brush it off. Keep a journal or spreadsheet of the "reach" suggestions. If I serve people who buy appliances I have to recognize other interrelated products. Cook wear. A niche fashion can be a really cool way for a home chef to feel more empowered. I can either brand them myself or simply resell other hot brands. Utensils like spatulas are another easy to execute merchandising pieces . Knives. Holy cow, do people spend a ton of money on knives! My new friends in the appliance community would love amazing knives at better prices, and I'm inclined to hook them up! Even subscription based ideas like Blue Apron. A way to practice your culinary skills without having to pick up the groceries. And hey, our people are local. You could hire someone to buy the ingredients, box them, and deliver them and for fresh cooked, restaurant quality meals at home. That business could turn into a monster. Talk about community!

Let's talk about the ice cream shop. Ask your people in a giveaway, or a question post on Instagram. What other related services or products would you like us to provide? People love to tell you what you should do next! LISTEN to them! Leverage your social media engagement to your advantage. Aside from catered ice cream parties, there is more. The space next door opened up. What if we lease it and open a burger place? The two seem to go together. Or what about limited edition ice creams? Or what about an ice cream club? Subscription based businesses work well because they are predictable. How about merchandise? Ice cream graphics are fun and look great. Let's get matching tie-dye ice cream shirts for the whole family! Or maybe an ice cream cone onesie. I'm not full of ideas on this one, but your friends and customers will be. Someone will tell you their pairing, product, or need for one, that will spark your idea to create your expansion.

Some expansions will serve more people than the original business. When Amazon started in the late 1990s, they sold books. They were an online bookseller at a time when Barnes & Noble was the biggest bookseller. Over the course of twenty or so years they slowly expanded into the behemoth we know today. Do you even buy books on Amazon today? Maybe you do, but you buy everything from mailing tape to groceries to furniture at the click of a button and sometimes, it arrives within hours! Get it? Amazon does the first part of Communal Commerce so well that the Encourage part happens automatically because you talk to your friends and family, saying things like, "I cannot believe that my life has been taken over by Amazon." Remember Amazon Prime fulfillment buttons? They save you money when you auto renew on a product you use constantly. When you're near running out, they'll send you a new case. Talk about automation! I recently saw a mug at my local coffee shop that said "This mom runs on wine and Amazon Prime" and was handmade by a local craftsman! There's a famous comedian who has started an ongoing Instagram bit on opening his wife's Amazon boxes, and it's hilarious. Now these are engaged AF customers.

Can you imagine if Amazon subscribed to all of the principles of Communal Commerce? We would feel a whole lot better about giving them our money. Communal Commerce could turn Amazon from a faceless, sometimes evil, corporate conglomerate utility you cannot avoid, into a world changing movement. It all comes from communication between you and your clientele, though. Expansion is not necessary, but if you still have the desire to give more in order to get more, ask your people what they need and want. Ask them where they go when they leave you, and what they've been doing lately.

My success in creating this community based company is not hard. It requires little in the form of risk. And it certainly doesn't require a massive investment of millions of dollars. In fact, like I mentioned in the previous examples, you will find yourself spending a fraction of the marketing revenue of your competitors for more impactful and meaningful marketing that actually makes a difference in peoples' lives. And that's the key thing about this way of doing business too: if you're doing it right, the profits will come, but more importantly, you will make tons of new friends and a lot of people very very happy on a regular basis.

So remember to repeat SEEE at every step. Remind yourself that this is a whole new way of approaching business building, and something you will begin employing in all of your business decisions, not just a simple one-and-done, easy fix solution. This is a new way of thinking as an entrepreneur. Active communication. Community. Creating the engagement to keep the momentum going. You will start SEEEing opportunity every step of the way. Remember this one thing: Real Communal Commerce is a dialogue where as traditional businesses are a monologue. PEACE. And #weareprivada

Date: Wed, Jan 27, 2021 at 9:35 PM

Subject: Re: Thai tea

To: Privada Cigar Club

<info@privadacigarclub.com>

It means so much more knowing that it's from your private stash and not likely to come by soon again.

I was watching Privada top 5 video last night on YouTube while Grace my wife was reading. I pointed you (on screen) to her and said, "Brian is giving me 2 rare cigars from his private stash".

Grace being married to me (a cigar smoker) a good 14 years, understands how special 'rare 'and 'private stash 'is.

Brian, your friendship is extremely valued. And if we get ourselves to NY and Orlando next year (our last WDW trip was 2017) allow me the pleasure of 1. Returning the favor, 2. Having a great smoke out with you.

F.

"What is dangerous is not to evolve."

Jeff Bezos

Founder, Amazon

About the Author

Born on August 22, 1978 in Manhattan, NY and raised in Allentown PA, Brian Desind spent most of his life pursuing a music career as a singer songwriter/rapper. After honing his song writing skills at Sigma Sound Studios in Philadelphia, he returned to New York in his early twenties. Brian received several record deals over the span of a decade and even worked with LL Cool J. During this time Brian worked a plethora of jobs in a multitude of industries from finance and sales to technology and recruiting. Trained in sales by his uncle Jeff Desind who headed a bond trading sales program for the legendary financial firm Bear Sterns, Brian excelled. Upon exiting the music industry in 2011 after a brief stint as a touring musician, Brian moved to Florida and found his passion for entrepreneurship. Several successful endeavors later, Brian founded Privada Cigar Club, a premium cigar subscription company that revolutionized the cigar industry. Brian is passionate about the progress of business and the relationship businesses have with their consumers. Brian believes right now is a pivotal moment that will change the way businesses serve their consumers and how they sell, distribute and market their products.

Glossary of Terms

Authoritize

Making yourself the authority on a subject.

Back serve

Openly giving credit to the behind the scenes components of a business that the end consumer does not always know about. For example, manufacturers, employees, craftsmen, farmers, etc. An example of use: a restaurant listing the farms where ingredients in the menu were procured.

Engage

To become friends with.

Expand

Offering a wider range of your product or service.

Serve

Going above and beyond the typical level of customer service in any industry.

Real Communal Commerce

A way of doing business that harnesses the power of the community it creates to leverage a mutually beneficial outcome.